The Challenge of

CLEAN AIR

MARTIN J. GUTNIK

✦Science, Technology, and Society Series✦

ENSLOW PUBLISHERS, INC.

Bloy St. & Ramsey Ave.	P.O. Box 38
Box 777	Aldershot
Hillside, N.J. 07205	Hants GU12 6BP
U.S.A.	U.K.

to
NATASHA
a silent partner in the writing of this book

Library of Congress Cataloging-in-Publication Data

Gutnik, Martin J.
    The challenge of clean air / by Martin J. Gutnik
p. cm. —(Science, technology, and society series)

Includes bibliographical references.

    Summary: Explores the scientific, technological, and social background of
the many environmental problems plaguing our air and atmosphere.

ISBN 0-89490-272-5

    1. Air—Pollution—Juvenile literature. [1. Air—Pollution.]
I. Title. II. Series: Science, technology, and society series (Hillside, N.J.)
TD883.13.G86 1990
363.73'92—dc20

Printed in the United States of America

10 9 8 7 6 5 4 3 2 1

Line Drawings Credit:
James A. Wiemer
Photograph Credits:
Jim Escalante, State of Wisconsin, Department of Natural Resources, 45; Staber
Reese, State of Wisconsin, Department of Natural Resources, 7; State of Wiscon-
sin, Department of Natural Resources, 16, 33, 44, 47; Dean Tvedt, State of
Wisconsin, Department of Natural Resources, 24, 26, 36
Cover Credit:
Dean Tvedt, State of Wisconsin, Department of Natural Resources

Contents

Introduction

On Friday, April 26, 1986, the citizens of Pripyat, in the Soviet Union, were awakened by two small explosions. Nobody knew then what had caused these explosions, and after they occurred, everything seemed quiet. That morning, life continued as usual. Men and women went to work, and children went to school. It wasn't until later in the day that a voice on the radio told them to go straight home and listen to the news for further developments.

The people of Pripyat did not know the nuclear power plant at Chernobyl had exploded, releasing radioactive poisons into the atmosphere. On Saturday, April 27, buses were sent into the town to evacuate its ten thousand inhabitants. The worst nuclear disaster in history was well underway.

On Sunday, April 28, the Soviet government released the first news story of the explosions. The story related that two workers had been killed in an accident at the Chernobyl plant. While the Soviet press played down the incident, the world press described it as a massive disaster, reporting thousands of deaths, confusion, panic, and large-scale evacuations. These first reports were very exaggerated and inaccurate, but they did draw attention to what was happening at Chernobyl. The world now focused on the incident. All watched and waited as the events began to unfold.

On May 12, 1986, the Soviet press reported that twenty-eight people had died in the disaster. It also related the seriousness of the accident to the Soviet people while, at the same time, attempting to minimize the dangers and potentially devastating effects.

Fallout (radioactive by-product) from the Chernobyl reactor explosion was deposited throughout the Northern Hemisphere, but its major impact was felt in Scandinavia. Winds carried the airborne poisons from Chernobyl around the globe, while rain washed the contaminants down to the earth. Because of the rains, Sweden and Norway experienced the highest levels of fallout.

What was in the rain was radioactive cesium 137, a waste product of a nuclear explosion. Radioactive cesium 137 has a half-life of thirty years. This means that if, for example, one ton of this material fell to the earth, in thirty years one-half of this would convert to an inactive state, leaving half a ton. In another thirty years, one-half of this would convert, and so on. In essence, it will take approximately twenty to thirty years for the radioactive cesium to reach safe levels, and approximately 120 years to become totally nonradioactive.

The effects of fallout on living things may be catastrophic. The contaminants are absorbed by plants and, through them, spread throughout the food chain. The food chain is the pattern of food relationships on earth. For example, corn becomes contaminated, cows eat the corn, and the milk produced by the cows is contaminated. People who drink this milk can be poisoned by the radioactive cesium.

In Scandinavia, especially Sweden and Norway, the reindeer were most immediately affected by the disaster at Chernobyl. Reindeer feed on lichens. A lichen is a combination of two plants, an alga and a fungus.

The lichen, because it has no root system, absorbs all its nutrients from the air. Because of this, lichens absorbed much more radioactive cesium 137 than other plants. The reindeer, which feed exclusively on lichens, thus became contaminated.

In Sweden and Norway, there live a group of nomadic people called the Sami. Traditionally, the Sami have earned their living from herding reindeer, and the reindeer once supplied the Sami with most of their needs. Today, the reindeer supply the Sami with money to live in the modern world. The contamination of the reindeer by the Chernobyl accident spells economic disaster for the Sami. Because of the high levels of reindeer contamination, many herds had to be slaughtered. The animals that escaped the slaughter may give birth to genetic freaks. The future looks glum for the Sami.

Chernobyl is but one incident in today's world that threatens

Smoke and vapor rise over a power plant. Note the blackened snow.

national economies, quality of life, and perhaps even life itself. All things in nature are interrelated. The air we breathe in the United States today may be breathed by Europeans two days from now and Asians a week later. Although nature cleanses many pollutants from the air, much of it remains polluted. Air pollution is one of the major problems facing the citizens of the modern world. How we deal with this problem will have a major impact on the future of human life on earth.

Today, the quality of the earth's air can be seen as both good and bad depending upon where one lives. Some cities, such as Denver, Colorado, and Mexico City, Mexico, still have severe air pollution problems, while others, such as Charleston, West Virginia, meet the clean air standards set by the United States federal government. Air pollution now plagues almost every major city in the United States, as well as many parts of the countryside.

Some of the major air pollution problems facing the earth are photochemical smog, a condition arising from the interaction of chemicals in the air with light; global warming, a condition caused by excess gases in the air trapping heat and preventing it from rising into space; depletion of the ozone layer, a condition caused by chlorofluorocarbons, chemical compounds used as propellants for aerosol spray cans, and halons, chemicals used in firefighting equipment, rising into the stratosphere, combining with the ozone layer and changing it into chlorine gas; and acid rain, caused by gases in the air, especially sulfur dioxide gas (SO_2), combining with water vapor and forming sulfurous acid. Solutions to these problems are very complicated. A basic understanding of science, technology, and society will give you a broad base with which to consider air pollution and to think what can be done about it.

The Science of Air
and Air Pollution

The word *atmosphere* refers to the primary layer of gases surrounding the earth. The atmosphere extends approximately 600 miles (965 kilometers) above the earth's surface. It exerts 14.7 pounds of pressure per square inch at sea level.

There are four major layers to the atmosphere. The layer of gases closest to the earth is called the troposphere. It is in the troposphere that the mixture of gases is just right for life as we know it to exist. Weather also occurs in the troposphere. The troposphere extends to ten miles above the earth's surface.

From ten to forty miles above the earth is the stratosphere. The stratosphere contains the protective ozone layer that surrounds the earth. Ozone is a form of oxygen which in the stratosphere blocks the harmful rays of the sun from reaching the surface of the earth.

Above the stratosphere is the thermosphere, or ionosphere. The ionosphere extends from fifty to three hundred miles above the earth's surface. In this layer, gases of the atmosphere are broken into individual electrically charged particles called ions. Because these ions reflect electromagnetic waves, the ionosphere plays an important role in long-distance radio communication. Radio waves bounce off the ionosphere's lower layer and travel for long distances. Another phenomenon that occurs in the ionosphere is the aurora borealis, or northern lights. An aurora is the result of particles from the sun coming into contact with the magnetic field of the earth. This contact produces a fantastic, dazzling display of light.

Above the ionosphere is the exosphere. The exosphere begins at three hundred miles above the earth's surface. It contains almost none of the gases found within the troposphere.

In this book, the word *air* will refer to the colorless, odorless, and tasteless mixture of gases found closest to the earth's surface, in the troposphere.

The Nature of Air

Two gases, nitrogen (N) and oxygen (O), make up 99 percent of the

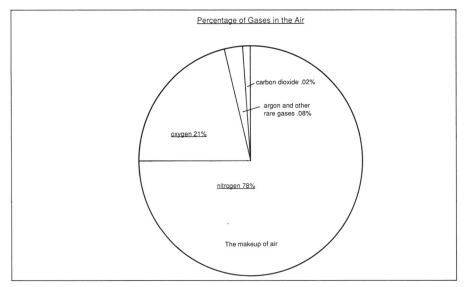

Percentage of Gases in the Air

carbon dioxide .02%

argon and other rare gases .08%

oxygen 21%

nitrogen 78%

The makeup of air

The air we breathe is composed of many different gases. Though we depend upon it for oxygen, air is mainly composed of nitrogen.

air. The other 1 percent of gases found in the air is nearly all argon. The remainder is carbon dioxide, .035%, and rare gases.

Air is transparent and has density (body). It has weight and takes up space. Because air possesses these physical qualities, it is matter. If you have ever blown up a balloon, you have seen that air takes up space. To demonstrate that air has weight, fill two balloons with an equal amount of air and tie them to a balance. A balance can be made of a yardstick and string. After the balloons are tied to each end, move the string in the middle of the yardstick until the balloons balance (see diagram). Pop one of the balloons with a pin, and the balance will move in the direction of the filled balloon.

Air is essential for life on earth to exist. Nitrogen and oxygen, the two most plentiful gases in the air, each provides a different ingredient for the existence of life. Nitrogen is essential in the formation of amino acids, the main ingredients of protein molecules.

All living things are made up of amino acids. Although there is

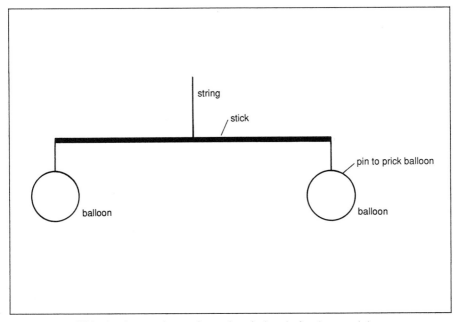

This simple experiment shows that air does in fact have weight.

plenty of nitrogen in the air, it cannot be used in the form of a gas by living things. So the nitrogen in the air must be converted into nitrogen compounds that can then be used by organisms (living things) to help make amino acids. Nitrogen gas in the air is converted into nitrogen compounds through a process known as the nitrogen cycle.

Oxygen is an extremely active gas, so it is readily transferable for use by organisms. Almost all living things need oxygen to exist. The exception to this rule is anaerobic bacteria, bacteria that can function without oxygen.

Oxygen is added to the air through photosynthesis. Photosynthesis is the process by which green plants make food. Green plants use

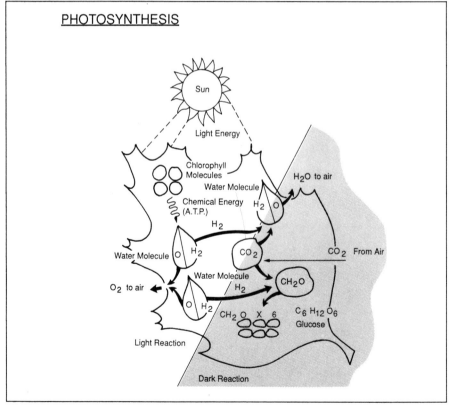

Plants produce oxygen through photosynthesis.

carbon dioxide (CO_2) and water (H_2O) in the presence of light energy to make glucose ($C_6H_{12}O_6$), a simple sugar. Oxygen gas (O_2) is produced as a by-product of the photosynthetic process and released into the air through the leaves of the plant.

Air is constantly moving around the earth. Air moves in two ways, wind and convection. Wind is caused by the sun, which creates weather systems in the troposphere. Convection is the manner in which air rises and falls, depending upon air temperature. Cold air, which is heavier than warm air, falls and, as it falls, it pushes the warmer, lighter air up.

Movement of the air is an important factor in keeping the air free of pollutants. It is in stagnant air that pollution becomes isolated and localized. In a temperature inversion, a body of warmer air moves over cooler surface air. When this happens, convection cannot take place and the air easily becomes polluted.

During a temperature inversion, the polluted, stagnant air is especially harmful to people with respiratory problems, older people, and very young people. The pollutants, such as nitrous oxide, nitrogen dioxide, carbon monoxide, and ozone, get into people's lungs and can cause damage to the lung tissue and to the sensitive linings of the nose. These pollutants and others also cause itching and burning of the eyes, sneezing, and severe allergic responses in people who suffer from allergies.

Air and the Heating of the Earth

The planet Earth is the only planet in the entire solar system with a balance of solar energy input and energy output. Because of certain gases in our atmosphere, specifically carbon dioxide (CO_2), the earth has a moderate temperature of 15° C (59° F). Without CO_2, the earth's average surface temperature would be only −17.8° C (0° F). This balance, between solar energy and energy returned to space, is achieved through radiation, convection, and conduction.

The sun radiates energy, which comes to the earth, where it is absorbed and converted into heat to warm the earth's surface. Actually, only a very small portion of the sun's energy reaches the earth's surface, the rest being lost in space or blocked by elements in the earth's atmosphere. Ozone, found in the stratosphere, blocks the sun's ultraviolet radiation.

Once the sun's energy has been absorbed by the earth, it is distributed to all parts of the globe through the processes of convection and conduction and water vapor. As heat from the surface of the earth rises, its escape is blocked by water vapor and other gases, such as CO_2. This helps to keep the surface of the earth warm. This process is often referred to as the greenhouse effect.

The air is also warmed by convection, the rising and falling of currents in the air; and conduction, heat transfer through the molecules of solid objects. Both convection and conduction help to distribute the heat from the sun around the earth.

Types of Air Pollutants

There are three basic types of air pollutants: gaseous, particulate, and aerosol. Gaseous pollution is any unnatural gas that is put into the air. Particulate pollution is caused by particles that float in the air. Aerosol pollution is particles that are so small and light that they stay afloat in the air for many years.

Particulate pollution of the air comes from a variety of sources. A great many of these sources are found in nature and are referred to as natural pollutants. Nature emits billions of tons of dust, aerosols, and particulates into the air every year. These pollutants are carried by the wind and convection currents throughout the atmosphere. More particulate and aerosol pollution comes from the activities of people. Industry, power generation, mining, transportation, and construction are sources of particulate air pollution.

There are four major types of gaseous pollutants of the air: carbon-based gases, sulfur-based gases, ozone, and nitrogen-based gases. Even small amounts of these gases can contaminate the air.

Water vapor in the air combines with many of these gases to form the acids that make up acid rain.

Carbon dioxide (CO_2) gas is found naturally in the air. But because of people's burning of fossil fuels (coal, oil, and natural gas), especially over the past century, many scientists fear that the increase in the levels of this gas will upset the temperature balance of the earth through the greenhouse effect.

Carbon monoxide (CO) is a colorless, odorless, and tasteless gas that is emitted into the air through the process of incomplete combustion of fossil fuels. Incomplete combustion occurs when fossil fuels are not burned at a high enough temperature and therefore are not completely consumed. Carbon monoxide is a deadly gas that, when inhaled (breathed in), combines with the hemoglobin (a chemical in red blood cells which carries oxygen) of red blood cells and renders them incapable of carrying oxygen. When red blood cells do not carry oxygen, the brain suffocates in a matter of minutes.

Sulfur dioxide (SO_2) is a colorless, tasteless, foul-smelling, heavier-than-air gas that occurs naturally, for example, from the activity of volcanoes or from the decomposition of organic (living) material in swamps. It is also produced by the burning of sulfur-containing fossil fuels. Sulfur dioxide combines with water vapor in the air, forming sulfurous acid (H_2SO_3), a major component of acid rain.

Ozone (O_3) is a form of oxygen and a major air pollutant. It is a very harsh irritant to the lungs and can be a serious problem for people with lung disorders.

Ozone in the atmosphere, however, is good. In the stratosphere, ozone acts as a filter to the sun's harmful rays. Without this ozone layer in the stratosphere, too many of these harmful rays can reach the earth's surface, causing skin cancer in humans and damage to plant tissues.

Photochemical air pollution is produced when gases emitted from natural sources, automobiles, and industries are involved in chemical reactions caused by sunlight. The ingredients of photochemical air pollution are ozone, a group of compounds called PAN, nitrogen oxide (NO), and nitrogen dioxide (NO_2).

Nitric oxide and nitrogen dioxide are produced by the incomplete combustion of gasoline. They combine with oxygen and, in the presence of light energy and hydrocarbons, form PAN, or peroxyacetyl nitrate. These oxides of nitrogen also combine with water vapor in the air, forming nitric acid (HNO_3), a component of acid rain. Another gas found in photochemical air pollution is ozone. Sulfur dioxide, carbon monoxide, and carbon dioxide are often present, but they are not photochemical.

Particles are another problem associated with photochemical smog. These particles are an irritant to the eyes and lungs.

Natural pollution of the atmosphere, in conjunction with people-made pollutants, contributes greatly to the air pollution

High ozone levels can be a serious health hazard to people with breathing problems. Here, in Milwaukee, Wisconsin, a sign was erected to warn people about dangerously high levels.

problems of today's world. Nature—as well as people—puts harmful gases, particles, and aerosols into the air.

During a drought, the soil becomes very dry, and on any windy day, particles and aerosols from this dry earth can be blown for miles. These particulates float in the air and are inhaled by people and other animals. Some of these particles, especially those from animal dung, can cause disease and other problems.

Plants also pollute the air. The foul odor from bogs and swamps is hydrogen sulfide (H_2S) gas, which smells like rotten eggs, and which can make people sick if they inhale too much of it. The pleasant odors from flowers are also a form of air pollution. Remember, air is an odorless substance. So any odor in the air, whether it is pleasant or not, is a form of pollution.

Plants also put particles and aerosols into the air. Some particles, such as pollen, ragweed, and mold, may cause eye and nose irritation.

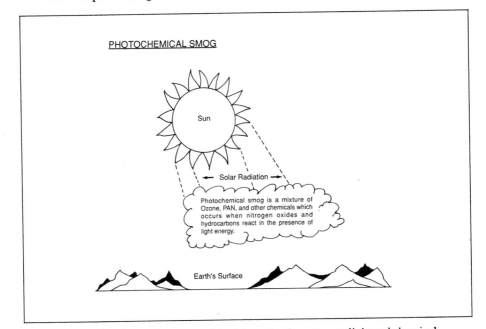

Photochemical smog is a result of the interaction between sunlight and chemicals in the atmosphere.

Some people have problems breathing if their allergies to plant substances are severe.

Volcanoes are also contributors to air pollution. Active volcanoes, such as Mount St. Helens, spew millions of tons of particles and aerosols into the air when they erupt. These particles, borne by the wind, spread over thousands of miles, causing breathing problems to people and other animals.

The particles also create an effective sun block by reflecting the light rays back into the stratosphere. In blocking the sun, these particles prevent the process of photosynthesis, thus harming the plant life that is affected. After the larger particles settle back to earth, the aerosols remain in the air.

Sulfur dioxide (SO_2) is the gas emitted from volcanoes. This gas is propelled thousands of feet into the air and is then borne by the wind and convection currents to many parts of the planet. Many scientists believe that the sulfur dioxide gas from volcanoes is a significant contributor to acid rain and global warming.

Forest Fires

Forest fires, like volcanoes, emit particulates, aerosols, and harmful gases into the air. These pollutants, propelled by the heat of the blaze, travel thousands of feet into the air and are then dispersed by the wind. Tons of carbon dioxide and carbon monoxide gases, as well as carbon soot and other particulates, are released into the air each year by forest fires.

Today, especially in the tropics, the problem of forest fires is worsening. In Brazil, for example, scientists say that the fires are so vast that they possibly account for one-tenth of the global output of carbon dioxide. Carbon dioxide gas is suspected of causing a warming of the earth through the greenhouse effect.

Global Warming

Carbon dioxide (CO_2) plays an important role in regulating the earth's temperature. Its molecules permit the passage of the shorter waves of solar radiation through the atmosphere, but interfere with the longer waves of heat radiating from the earth's surface. Because of carbon dioxide's ability to block heat loss, if there is too much carbon dioxide in the air, heat cannot escape. This is the greenhouse effect. The heat can enter but not escape.

Due to the increase of carbon dioxide in the air, many scientists believe that the earth's temperature is on the rise. This is referred to as global warming, and its results could be devastating. Any significant rise in the earth's temperature might cause the arctic ice cap to melt. If this happens, many of the earth's coastal cities, such as New Orleans, New York, San Francisco, Vancouver, and Singapore, could be endangered. A change in temperature will also cause significant

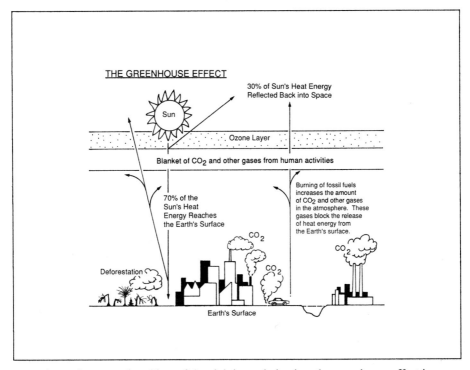

An environmental problem of the eighties and nineties, the greenhouse effect is caused by human activities.

changes in specific ecosystems, specialized parts of the earth, such as ponds, lakes, and forests.

Emissions from the earth's forest fires, especially those in the Amazon region, along with CO_2 emissions from industry, especially the burning of coal for power generation, travel thousands of miles. Some scientists believe there is a direct link between these harmful emissions, along with chlorofluorocarbons, and the damage to the earth's ozone shield over Antarctica. Gases from these fires rise 12,000 feet into the air and are carried even higher by jet streams. Experts believe that several of the gases emitted from these fires, such as methane (CH_4) and nitrogen oxides, are among the reactive gases that can deplete the earth's protective ozone layer, allowing harmful rays from the sun to reach the surface of the earth.

The Biosphere

Life on earth exists in a delicate balance of the living and nonliving environments. Both the living and nonliving aspects of the planet interrelate to create what is known as the biosphere, anywhere life can exist.

The living aspect of the biosphere is referred to as biological, while the nonliving aspects are referred to as physical. There are only four physical aspects to the biosphere: water, soil (sand, gravel, rock, clay, etc.), air, and light energy.

The study of how all living things interrelate with each other and their nonliving environment is known as ecology. Every aspect of these various interrelationships is critical in maintaining the delicate balance necessary for life on earth to exist. As the balance of the atmosphere becomes damaged by the activities of nature and people, life on this planet becomes more precarious.

We must find ways of living in conjunction with nature in order to stop the destruction of our atmosphere. Our future depends on it.

Technology
and Industry

Technology is the application of science to industry, commerce, and transportation. Approximately one-third of the earth's population today lives in a high-technology society, while the other two-thirds live in societies struggling to become highly technological.

Effects of Technology on the Environment

The environment is rapidly changing, too. With more cars, trucks, and buses comes congestion in the cities and on the freeways. More jet airplanes bring more noise and larger airports. With more industry comes more contamination of the air and water. With more products comes more waste. Where will we put it all?

As ecology is the interaction of the forces of nature, so is the problem of the human environment. Three factors combine to create the environmental problems of today's world. One is the burst of human population on this planet. Human overpopulation may be the single most prominent factor in reducing the quality of life on earth.

Second is the lack of a systematized program for land use

worldwide for the benefit of the environment and people. For this reason, we have farmers burning the rain forests of South America and land speculators destroying the wilderness in Canada.

Finally, and most important, there is the narrow use of technology to achieve progress without consideration of its impact on the natural and human environmental condition. More often than not, people consider themselves separate from or above the natural order of things. Because of human dominance, people have developed a chauvinistic attitude toward all living things in nature. The earth, some believe, was created for our benefit, and, therefore, we can do as we wish on this planet.

It is easy to forget that we are part of nature and the natural order of things. Our bread, rice, vegetables, and fruits come from plants, which depend upon the soil. The soil itself was made fertile over generations of interrelationships and changes. The meat we eat comes from animals dependent upon plants, or dependent on other animals that eat plants for food.

All things in nature are interrelated, including people. It is the disruption of this delicate balance that endangers life on earth.

Through advanced technology, people have improved their quality of life and, at the same time, because of a lack of understanding, or simply not caring, have created significant environmental disruptions. Nature pollutes the atmosphere, but people, through technology, increase this pollution tenfold. There are five major ways people pollute the air: transportation; industry and power plants; chemicals and aerosols; nuclear energy; and home and industrial heating.

Transportation

Any person who lives in a major metropolitan area in the world has witnessed the air pollution problems caused by the transportation system. Since the beginning of human society, transportation has always been a problem and a necessity for people. Early societies found it advantageous to locate urban areas on waterways to transport goods and people. The Romans built highways to connect the far reaches of their empire to the capital.

With the coming of the Industrial Revolution, more and more people crowded into the cities. Cities grew unchecked, more goods were produced, and markets for these goods were developed. A major problem was how to move the goods to the various markets and how to transport the workers to the factories. In answer to this, land-based mass transportation systems were developed. First came the railroads, then the trolleys, and, finally, the subways.

People, however, especially in Western cultures, demanded more comfort and convenience. As a result, there was a shift from these mass transport systems to the family automobile. Today, it is the multitude of individually owned vehicles that contributes most to the earth's air pollution problems.

The basic fuel for all major forms of transportation is gasoline.

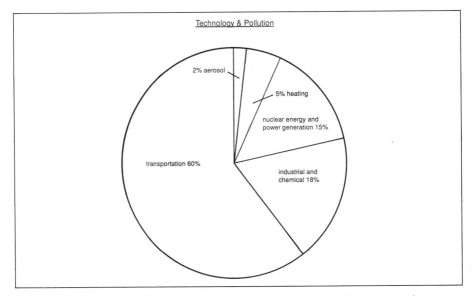

The major source of pollutants emitted into the atmosphere is transportation. Finding ways to make transportation "cleaner" could greatly reduce air contamination.

Gasoline is a volatile mixture of flammable liquid hydrocarbons, which is derived chiefly from crude petroleum, which is a fossil fuel. A fossil fuel is derived from the compressed or liquefied remains of plants and animals that lived millions of years ago.

Gasoline for transportation is burned in the internal combustion engine. This engine works by igniting the fuel internally, using it to turn the drive shaft that powers the vehicle. The major problem with the internal combustion engine is that it does not burn the fuel at high enough temperatures and, thus, does not burn the fuel completely. When fuel is not burned completely, the process is referred to as incomplete combustion.

Complete combustion of gasoline would result in the release into the air of carbon dioxide, heat, and water vapor, none of which is a toxic pollutant, although the emission of carbon dioxide has been

Our society is dependent on fossil-fueled transportation.

linked to the greenhouse effect, which is responsible for global warming.

Incomplete combustion of gasoline at high temperatures results in the formation of several emissions which, when released into the air, react with the ultraviolet light from the sun, and form the compounds that make up photochemical smog: PAN, nitric oxide (NO), nitrogen dioxide (NO_2), carbon monoxide (CO), and ozone (O_3).

Automobiles and other forms of transportation also put millions of tons of particles into the air annually. Among these particles may be traces of nickel (Ni), lead (Pb), copper (Cu), or any of the other additives that are in gasoline. These particles, when inhaled, can be harmful.

Industrial Pollution

Particulate pollution of the air, in the form of dust or smoke and sulfur dioxide (SO_2), is a major form of industrial pollution. These particles and gases are being released into the atmosphere in ever-increasing quantities because of the increasing number of industries worldwide. The particles range from the very fine dust from cement and fertilizer factories; to chemicals used in the production of foam containers and other paper industry products; to emissions from steel factories, smelting factories, and many other factories of different kinds.

Many researchers believe we are adding new chemical pollutants to the air faster than we can identify them or recognize their hazards. Then, as was the case with chlorofluorocarbons, which destroy the ozone layer, when we finally discover the disasters that can occur from these chemicals, it is often too late to repair the damage that has been done.

In the Soviet Union, at least fifty million people live in areas where the air pollution levels are at least ten times the minimum levels set for health quality by the Soviet government. The air is so dirty that by midsummer, many of the tree leaves are covered with a fine dust. This reduces the process of photosynthesis and results in reduced growth, and may eventually kill the trees. Many Soviet factories, unchecked, emit hundreds of thousands of tons of poisonous substances into the air every year.

In the United States, federal standards have been set for industrial emissions. Although there is still a significant amount of particulate and SO_2 pollution, it is not as uncontrolled as in the Soviet Union.

Chemicals and Their Effect on the Ozone Layer

Recent changes in the ozone layer have many scientists very worried. In March 1988, the National Aeronautics and Space Administration (NASA) reported on a study it made of the ozone layer. The study verified that the earth's ozone layer has been depleted by 3 percent over the past twenty years.

Halons are chemicals used in high-technology fire-fighting

Smoke pouring from smokestack of paper mill. The paper industry is a major source of particulate matter.

equipment. Chlorofluorocarbons (CFCs) are a group of chemical compounds which were widely used as propellants for aerosol spray cans and are still used in plastics packaging, foam insulation, cleaning fluids, air conditioning, and refrigeration. These halons and chlorofluorocarbons, once released into the air, rise slowly into the atmosphere, where they and methyl chloroform, an industrial solvent, are broken up by the sun's ultraviolet rays, releasing chlorine (Cl) and bromine (Br) atoms. The chlorine atoms from CFCs and bromine from halons disrupt the ozone molecules, breaking them up into molecular oxygen. This depletes the ozone layer. Without this ozone layer, life as we know it on earth would be impossible.

The decrease in the ozone layer creates many problems for living things. For example, every 1 percent loss of ozone increases the potential for human skin cancers by 5 to 7 percent. The increased radiation from the sun also burns the tissues of animals and plants, as well as causing eye problems for humans and other animals. Most dangerous might be changes in the human immune system. The immune system protects your body from disease.

The increased ultraviolet radiation has also affected the food chain. The radiation appears to kill plankton, tiny organisms that live in the ocean. Plankton is at the base of the food chain, which means many other organisms depend upon it as a source of food. With reduced amounts of plankton, there will be less food for ocean fish. This will eventually result in less and less fish for human consumption.

The greatest loss to the earth's ozone shield has occurred over Antarctica where, in the winter and early spring months, the ozone layer has been measured to decrease up to 50 percent. Scientists often refer to this area of loss as the ozone hole. Some researchers fear that ozone losses, like the one over Antarctica, may begin to occur over other areas of the earth as well.

Chemicals and Air Pollution

Persistent chemicals are those that do not break down readily in the natural environment. These chemicals, which are put into the air via chemical plants, spraying, and other industrial sources, are almost impossible to clean up, as they work their way into the food chain and are passed from one living thing to another.

Chemical pesticides such as DDT, which is not now in use in the United States, and other chlorinated hydrocarbons are released into the air, where they remain until washed to the ground by rain or deposited by gravity. Once on the ground, these chemicals invade the ecosystem and remain part of the environment for years. Only recently have we begun to comprehend the effects of these compounds.

Fossil Fuels

The major fuels used by industry worldwide today are oil and coal. Oil is used a great deal more than coal. Both of these are fossil fuels. Oil comes from the remains of tiny plants and animals that once

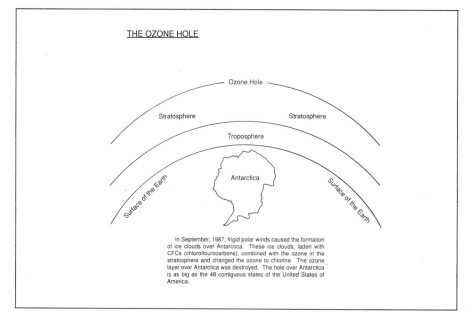

THE OZONE HOLE

Ozone Hole

Stratosphere   Stratosphere

Troposphere

Antarctica

Surface of the Earth   Surface of the Earth

In September, 1987, frigid polar winds caused the formation of ice clouds over Antarctica. These ice clouds, laden with CFCs (chloroflourocarbons), combined with the ozone in the stratosphere and changed the ozone to chlorine. The ozone layer over Antarctica was destroyed. The hole over Antarctica is as big as the 48 contiguous states of the United States of America.

The ozone hole over Antarctica has become a major concern of people everywhere.

lived in shallow seas millions of years ago. Over time, these seas dried up or were covered over with deeper water. These organisms, because their remains were buried in the muck at the bottom, did not decompose. Instead, their bodies were compressed until, over the years, they turned into oil.

Coal comes from the remains of swampy forests which existed millions of years ago. When trees died in these forests, they would fall into the mucky bottom. Because oxygen could not reach them, they did not decompose. Over the ages, these forests were covered over by other layers, and were compressed into what today is known as coal.

Both coal and oil have been potential air pollutants from the time they were first brought out of the ground. The mining techniques themselves are great contributors to destruction of the natural environment. For example, strip mining for coal, up until very recently, usually left the land scarred and barren. Because there was no vegetation left after the miners departed, the soil was eroded by the wind and rain.

The major problem with coal and oil, however, is in the manner in which they are burned for energy. With today's technology, complete combustion is not really feasible.

Both coal and oil contain large amounts of sulfur. As these fuels are burned, the sulfur is released into the air as sulfur dioxide gas (SO_2). Environmental scientists today believe that there is no longer any question that emissions of sulfur dioxide produce acid rain, and that acid rain harms the environment by changing the pH levels (acidity) of lakes and by destroying plant tissues.

In conjunction with sulfur emissions, the oxides of nitrogen, (NO) and (NO_2), are also contributors to the acid rain problem. These oxides of nitrogen, as stated earlier, are derived mostly from automobile combustion of gasoline. Combined, the sulfur dioxide and nitrogen oxides represent a great threat to the natural environment, especially the lakes.

Acid Rain

The pH scale is used for measuring the level of acidity, or alkalinity, of various substances. According to this scale, any substance that has a pH of 7.0 is neutral; below 7.0 is acid; and above 7.0 is basic, or alkaline.

Most rainwater is naturally acid (approximately 5.6 to 6.6 on the pH scale), because the water, as it falls through the air, absorbs carbon dioxide gas (CO_2), thus forming carbonic acid (H_2CO_3). This weak acid is often referred to as soft water. Acid rain has a pH of from approximately 3.9 to 4.6 on the pH scale.

The formula for destruction of the environment is as follows: sulfur dioxide (SO_2) and oxides of nitrogen, (NO) and (NO_2), are released into the air from transportation and industry. In industry, the culprits are mainly coal and oil-fired plants, smelters, and boilers.

Today, the amounts of sulfur dioxide and oxides of nitrogen emitted from these sources are very large. In the United States and

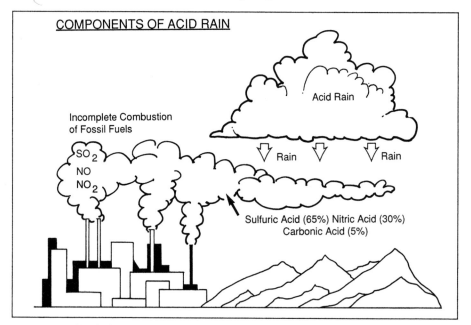

Acid rain is created from sulfuric and nitric acids produced by industry.

Canada combined, over thirty million tons of sulfur dioxide are released into the air annually. Along with Europe, Japan, and the rest of the industrialized world, over 100 million tons of SO_2 and over eighty million tons of NO and NO_2 are pumped into the atmosphere annually.

These pollutants are borne by the wind, reacting with other substances (gases, particles, and water vapor) to be converted from gases to acids. The gases react with moisture in the air to form the acid compounds found in acid rain. Particulates and aerosols of nitric and sulfurous acid that remain in the air are eventually deposited in forests, buildings, and crop lands.

Once the acid rain falls to the soil, it becomes part of the hydrologic cycle (water cycle). As the raindrops percolate (bubble) through the soil, because of their acid content, they leach (absorb)

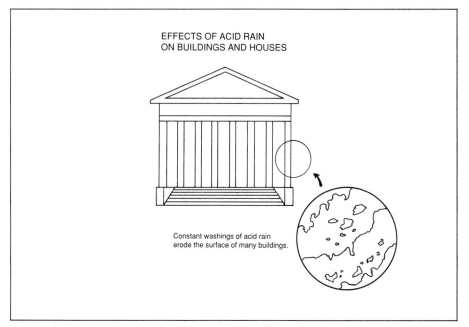

EFFECTS OF ACID RAIN
ON BUILDINGS AND HOUSES

Constant washings of acid rain
erode the surface of many buildings.

Acid rain corrodes marble and limestone, which have been used for centuries to build monuments and public buildings.

metals and other substances contained in the soil, carrying these with them to the lakes or groundwater pools, where they stay.

It is in these lakes and pools, especially in Scandinavia and the eastern sections of the United States and Canada, that scientists have observed the most devastating effects from acid rain. In Scandinavia, thousands of lakes have been affected, the acid pollution eliminating the fish, plankton, and other forms of life. Only acid-tolerant organisms, such as the water boatman beetle and a few other insects, plus certain forms of aquatic life, can exist in an acid lake.

Acid lakes are not dead lakes, but the pH level has been so changed that the lakes cannot support the life that existed there for thousands, if not millions, of years. For example, in many of the Adirondack lakes and ponds of Canada and New York, the brook trout have vanished. Communities have attempted stocking these once fertile lakes, but to no avail. The acid content of the water is now too high to support most kinds of fish.

People, too, are affected by the acid rain. The acidified groundwater is pumped into wells. The acid leaches the chemicals from the metal in the pipes, causing damage to the system, and possible harm to the users. One of the chemicals leached from copper pipes is copper sulfate ($CuSO_4 \cdot 5H_2O$). Copper sulfate turns the water green so that, when people wash their hair in this water, it too turns green. Other chemicals in large enough quantities can do great harm to human beings, sometimes causing death.

As well as the rain itself, the gases of acid rain have been shown to be associated with increased respiratory problems in people. People with chronic bronchitis, asthma, and emphysema are the most greatly affected. Researchers estimate that these airborne sulfates and nitrates are responsible for over 120,000 deaths a year worldwide.

Nuclear Energy

In order to save energy and stave off the effects of too much fossil fuel consumption, there has been a move by many countries in the world toward nuclear power plants. There are two kinds of nuclear power known to people today: fission and fusion. In fission reactors, the atom is split, creating a chain reaction of energy which releases tremendous amounts of heat and light. The process of nuclear fusion crushes the atom, also creating a chain reaction which releases vast amounts of heat and light.

Nuclear fusion, as an efficient source of energy for the world, is still in the infant stages of development. Fission, however, has been an alternative source of power since the end of World War II. The dangers from nuclear fission power plants lie in the radioactive waste products these plants produce and the chance of an accident, such as the one that occurred at Chernobyl.

Radiation occurs naturally in the environment. This radiation derived from radioactive elements in the environment is referred to as background radiation. No amount of radiation is good for living

Acid precipitation sampler.

things. Any extra radiation a person receives can be dangerous. Increased exposure to radiation is potentially harmful. Modern medical research has demonstrated that radiation does cause cancer, mutations, and many other maladies that can prove fatal to human beings.

Disposing of radioactive waste products from fission reactors has developed into a major environmental problem for today and the future. Waste materials stay radioactive for many years. Carbon 14, which occurs naturally in the environment and in all living things, has a half-life of 5,568 years. Strontium 90 and cesium 137, two dangerous isotopes, have half-lives of 28 and 33 years respectively. This means that 28 years after strontium 90 is put into the environment, one-half of it will become nonradioactive. In another 28 years, one-half of what is left will dissipate, and in another 28 years after that, one-half of what is still left will become nonradioactive, and so on. The effects of this element will be felt for approximately 100 years.

The waste products from nuclear reactors pose dangers to both the environment and civilization. For example, plutonium derived from these waste products can be used to make nuclear warheads. There is always the danger that some terrorist group will obtain some of this plutonium and use it to manufacture a nuclear device.

An even greater danger to the environment lies in the storage of these nuclear wastes. These by-products are stored in heavy lead containers and are buried either in the ground or under the sea. Knowing the persistence of these elements and the volatile nature of the earth, what guarantees do we have that an earthquake or some other natural disaster will not crack these containers, leaving the radioactive poison to seep into the groundwater or seawater?

Even more risky than the storage of nuclear wastes is the chance for another accident like that at Chernobyl. In this type of accident, the radioactive materials are spewed into the air and carried to all parts of the globe by wind and convection. The effects of this type of disaster will plague the earth for many years to come.

Technological Solutions, if Any

Since the beginning of scientific research, people have looked to it as a remedy for the problems of everyday life. However, more often than not, technological miracles have turned out to be more problematic than the problem they were created to solve.

Science and technology, when properly applied, can improve the living standards for people the world over. This happens only when the application of a new discovery is commenced with a broad perspective of the problem in general. With a narrow perspective, all too often the miracles of science and technology have turned out to be disasters.

The Technology of Pesticides

Pesticides were developed by scientists to protect agricultural crops and people from insect pests. The first of these to be developed, during World War II, was DDT. This chemical was touted as the answer to the problems of hunger and much disease.

In its first applications, DDT was used to combat the mosquito, which carried the disease malaria. Its success was almost instantaneous, as the number of United States servicemen and servicewomen exposed to the disease was greatly reduced. In response, the production and broad application of DDT was greatly increased, with little investigation into its side effects.

At first, the use of DDT wiped out malaria in many parts of the world by eliminating the mosquitoes that carried malaria. It also killed many crop-destroying insects, resulting in an instant increase in world crop yields. However, the researchers who developed this pesticide did not consider the complexity of the natural community. The first successes with DDT gave false hopes to the people using it. Although DDT wiped out most of the insect pests, it did not get them all. The insects that survived reproduced, with their offspring having more resistance to the chemical than the original community of insects.

Eventually, a population of mosquitoes and insect pests emerged that was completely resistant to DDT.

While these insects developed an immunity to DDT, other animal species, especially birds, did not fare so well. Because DDT is not soluble in water (does not dissolve) and, because it is persistent in the environment (does not break down readily), it remains active for many years after being applied.

Scientific studies have shown rains wash the DDT into rivers, streams, and lakes, where the chemical, ingested by aquatic organisms, becomes part of the food chain. The chemical is also absorbed by plants through their roots. Birds that eat the plants or fish ingest high levels of DDT into their bodies.

In living tissues, DDT does not break down into a harmless substance. In birds, the chemical is changed to DDE, a poisonous substance that prevents the birds from producing calcium carbonate,

Apple orchard being sprayed by machine.

the major ingredient of eggshells. Without enough calcium carbonate, the birds lay eggs without shells or with weakened shells. As a result, the eggs do not hatch. Thus, the birds cannot reproduce.

Not knowing these terrible consequences, farmers and communities used DDT in large amounts. It was not until 1962, when Rachel Carson published her best-seller *Silent Spring*, that people became aware of the awesome effects of this chemical.

Other Technological Attempts at Solutions

In spite of the DDT lesson and many others, people still look to technology to provide the solutions to most of their problems.

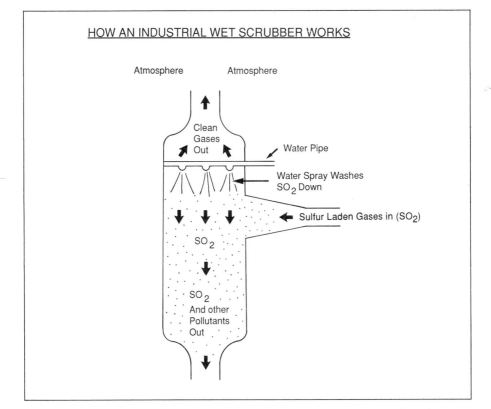

The wet scrubber has been created to produce cleaner emissions from factories and other industry.

Electrostatic precipitators were developed to reduce particulate pollution from the smokestacks of industries. Their results are quite impressive, as particulate pollution has been reduced by approximately thirty-three percent. The precipitators, however, cannot capture the very fine particles emitted. These chemicals escape from the chimneys of industry and remain in the air.

Technology and Energy

New technologies in energy could be an answer to many of our air pollution woes. Scientists are now looking to solar power and fusion as possible solutions to both the air pollution and energy consumption crisis.

At the present time, the world's average annual energy consumption is equal to approximately ten barrels of oil per person. This energy consumption, however, is not distributed equally among the inhabitants of the planet. Seventy percent of the earth's population

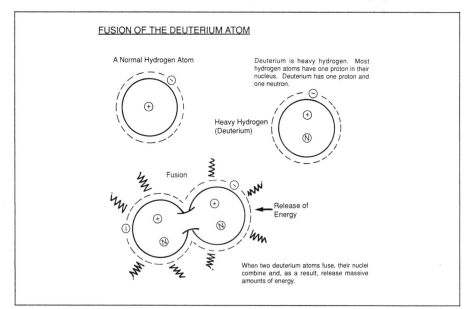

Researchers looking for a clean, efficient form of energy are hoping to discover the mystery of fusion.

is well below the ten-barrel-a-day average. In order to equalize consumption in the future so that all people have a high standard of living, we will require massive amounts of energy.

Since the Industrial Revolution, fossil fuels have been the major source of energy on earth. At the present rate of consumption, it is predicted that we will run out of fossil fuels by the middle of the twenty-first century.

Many energy researchers today are working on projects to capture solar energy from the sun. The solar energy that reaches the earth today is diffused (spread out) over a vast area. For this energy to be utilized by industry and power plants, it must be concentrated.

Some scientists have developed solar collectors to store and concentrate the sun's energy. These collectors are flat plates that absorb the sun's energy and store it in heated water. The heated water may be used for home heating and small power generators. As scientists improve the technology of these solar collectors, they may eventually be refined to produce the amount of energy required to run electric power plants.

As our scientists find more efficient ways to collect, concentrate, and store solar energy, it is possible that the sun may become a major source of people's energy on the planet Earth. This solar energy would be a totally clean, nonpolluting, inexhaustible source of energy to run factories, cities, and automobiles.

Another area of energy research today is the development of fusion. Fusion is a nuclear reaction in which the atom implodes (crushes). With the development of fusion power, the energy needs of the world could be solved for centuries to come.

Fusion energy is a desirable alternative to fission (splitting of the atom), because it produces virtually no radioactivity. The dangers of radioactivity to people were discussed earlier in this book. The major reason for the lack of radiation lies in the fuel used for the fusion reaction, He-3. He-3 is a compound, similar to the element helium. It is produced by the sun and carried by the solar winds all over the solar system. However, there is very little He-3 on earth.

It seems that if a planet or solar body has a gravitational field or atmosphere, the He-3 just goes around it. The earth has both a gravitational field and an atmosphere. Therefore, the particles of He-3 never make it to the surface of this planet.

The earth's moon has neither gravitation nor an atmosphere. Tons of He-3 have been piling up on the surface of the moon for centuries. Scientists estimate that there is approximately a million tons of He-3 on the moon's surface. It is predicted this is enough to provide fusion reactors with all their energy needs for the world for the next ten thousand years.

With the development of fusion reactors would come energy in a form that could be converted directly into electricity, with an efficiency factor estimated at 70 percent. This is extremely high. Fusion power would also make interplanetary space travel a real possibility for the future.

Most importantly, however, the development of fusion energy would immediately decrease our dependence on fossil fuels as a source of energy, and one day replace the use of fossil fuels. A direct result would be cleaner air, free of sulfur dioxide, carbon monoxide, and PAN, and with much less carbon dioxide.

Unfortunately, fusion and solar power alone will not solve our air pollution problems. There will still be chemical pollution, forest fires, radon, and pesticides. In truth, the answer lies with people. Only people can stop the pollution of the air. What it all comes down to is the human desire to live in a clean, well-functioning biosphere.

Society
and Air Pollution

Advances in technology have aided transportation and industry. Better emission controls have been developed for automobiles and scrubbers have been installed on the smokestacks of industries. Yet, in spite of these improvements, air pollution problems seem to be worsening. In the words of author Charles Dickens, it is "the best of times and the worst of times."

Many cities' air pollution problems have improved, while those of others, like Denver, Colorado, have worsened. Denver has a death rate for lung disease that is 30 percent higher than the national average. In Mexico City, Mexico, the houses and buildings are actually covered with a fine soot from the ever-present cloud of pollutants that hangs over the urban area.

In order to clean the air, tough, widespread measures are needed. The world will have to switch to mass transit instead of relying on the automobile. Every industry, large and small, will have to be monitored to keep tight control over its emissions. Is the public willing to pay this price? Are you?

Human Population Growth

For most of human existence, the population has probably remained under 5 million. With the development of agriculture, it became possible to feed even more people. By the time of Christ, the earth's population was up to about 135 million. It took another 1,500 years for the earth's population to reach 500 million.

Medical technology blossomed in the late nineteenth and early twentieth centuries. This technology, along with improved sanitary conditions, allowed the human population to burgeon. People lived longer, while infant mortality decreased. Suddenly, the world was filled with people.

People prospered worldwide, and between the years 1650 and 1850 the population doubled. There were now a billion people on earth. The human population doubled again in only eighty years, by 1930. Today, the earth has over 5 billion people, and some experts project that by the year 2000, there will be over 7 billion people, and by 2015, over 10 billion.

The continued technology of medicine and science has served the human population well, but it has also removed people from the natural environment. As long as the human population continues to grow unchecked, we will have a world in crisis. Every day 200,000 people are added to the world population.

Will technology continue to be able to respond to the needs and problems of 200,000 more mouths to feed daily? An elderly population? Loss of habitat for other living things? Housing for a world filled with people? Energy for this mass of humanity?

Air pollution in the 1990s will reach crisis proportions unless something is done to effectively reduce our air pollution woes. In many areas of the world, the quality of the air is already too low for the health of people and other organisms.

New evidence of a decrease in the earth's protective ozone layer cries out for a complete ban of chlorofluorocarbons, halons, and methyl chloroform. There is mounting evidence that the greenhouse effect is already affecting the earth's climate. The summer drought of 1988, in which many farmers lost crops and plants and wildlife suffered, has been linked to global warming. Global warming is likely to get worse, as long as carbon dioxide and other heat-trapping gases continue to be emitted into the atmosphere.

Air pollution is contributing heavily to the destruction of our forests, as well as causing billions of dollars of damage of crops. Unless these pollution levels are reduced, crop damage will increase. Pollution is getting so bad that the World Resources Institute, a Washington-based environmental research group, has called for a 50 percent reduction in sulfur dioxide emissions over the next ten years, and a 25 percent reduction in the emission of nitrogen oxide.

History of Pollution Control

Why then, in the presence of such strong evidence that the earth is in crisis, has so little been done to stem the effects of pollution? The problem is very complicated, so in order to understand why, we must go back and look at some of the history of attempts at pollution control.

By 1970, pollution was getting so terrible that the United States Congress passed the Clean Air Act. This law ordered the individual states to develop methods for reducing the amounts of pollutants being put into the air. The Act created the Environmental Protection Agency (EPA), which was to set safe air standards and monitor the state of the air.

Unfortunately, in spite of the Clean Air Act, air pollution continued to worsen. This led to the creation of concerned citizen groups, such as consumer and environmental advocates and other lobbying groups, who pressured both the government and private sectors to do something about air pollution.

Thanks largely to the efforts of these advocacy organizations, some progress was made. United States automakers were required to manufacture vehicles that burned fuel more efficiently, putting fewer harmful emissions into the air, but things were not better yet.

The earth was still endangered, as the brunt of people pollution was beginning to weigh even more heavily on the planet. The entire body of air encompassing the planet was polluted. People were getting sick and dying, as were forests, rivers, lakes, and oceans.

In 1977, the United States's Clean Air Act came up for renewal. At this time, most of the cities and manufacturers who were to have met the standards of the 1970 act had not. Instead of being punished for this, they were given extensions. The Clean Air Act of 1977 established clean air standards for all cities to meet by 1982. Again, in 1981, the United States Environmental Protection Agency extended the deadline, this time until December 31, 1987.

Collecting snow samples to determine the acidity of winter precipitation. The average pH of Wisconsin rain and snow has been found ten times more acidic than normal.

Still, many industries worldwide did not comply with minimal universal clean air standards. They complained and lobbied against these laws, stating that compliance would be too much of a financial burden upon them. Manufacturers are in business to make profits. If an industry must spend more to make its product because of air pollution controls, it will receive less profit or, in order to keep profits the same, the pollution control costs will be passed on to the consumer in the form of higher prices for the product. A good example of this is found in the automobile industry, where pollution controls have driven up the price of automobiles.

United States manufacturers claim that, because of the higher standards of the United States's Clean Air Act requirements, their manufacturing costs would become noncompetitive, since foreign producers do not have to meet these same standards. They argue that,

A scientist changing a filter in a high volume sampler.

due to the lower price because of lower production costs, the consumer would buy the foreign product. This leads some United States firms to threaten to close their doors. A coal-burning plant, rather than paying the cost of conversions to another cleaner fuel, closes. People who work in the plant lose their jobs. The government loses a source of tax revenue, and the general economy of the area decreases. Everyone is unhappy, as unemployment rises, along with taxes for public assistance programs.

This position becomes politicized when the people of any given community put more pressure on the government to clean up the air. The government responds by requiring industries to meet certain minimum standards. The industry, for reasons previously stated, refuses to comply, and threatens to leave the community if this pressure on it continues.

Out of fear of economic loss if the industry were to relocate, people ease their pressure on the government, and the government eases its pressures on industries and cities by extending its deadlines. The government does not want the industry to leave the community, because the industry provides many needed jobs. They also claim that people would be more upset about not having a job than about the quality of the air. It is a vicious circle: If the government enforces pollution control, the industries will leave; if the government does not enforce pollution control, people are unhappy over the quality of the air they must breathe.

On December 31, 1987, many cities of the United States had still failed to meet the minimum standards set by the renewal of the Clean Air Act for six air pollutants. Among the six pollutants were ozone, sulfur, and carbon monoxide. Once again Congress gave these cities, among them Los Angeles, Houston, Denver, Atlanta, and New York, another reprieve. They now had until August 31, 1988, to clean up their air to meet the EPA's minimum standards. Congress hoped that these cities would find the political will to act responsibly toward the environment.

August 1988 came and went, and still the air over many cities was as foul as before. Most cities had not even implemented such basic pollution-reducing measures as stricter controls on vehicle and power plant emissions. This time, however, the EPA named some of these cities to suffer sanctions, such as construction bans and cutoffs of highway funds.

Lee Thomas, the administrator of the EPA, said in 1988 that it was time for the EPA to move against the polluters. He put sanctions on cities like Denver, Atlanta, Dallas–Fort Worth, and Los Angeles. The question now becomes: Will the sanctions do anything? Many critics of the EPA say the sanctions have no teeth; that they do not take enough away to make it politically feasible for the cities to move against polluters.

In the spring of 1990, Congress was in the process of passing a revised Clean Air Act. This bill would have tougher standards. Deadlines to meet these new standards, however, would still be five or more years away.

Taking personal responsibility for keeping the environment pollution-free can begin with the family car.

The real solution seems to be in developing a new mass transit program, which would replace the family automobile as the main form of transportation, as well as extremely tight controls on industry and power generation.

Herein lies the paradox: To have breathable air, we need to revamp the entire system of transportation and industry worldwide. Laws punishing polluters will have to be severe, and individuals must be willing to make many personal sacrifices. People understand this but still resist attempts to take away their personal comforts, especially the automobile. What will be the outcome—clean air or more pollution?

Epilogue

With each passing year, the quality of the earth's air both improves and worsens. While science and technology make some advances in the war against pollution, they also create and discover other air pollution problems that the world was unaware of previously. Is there hope? Yes, but where does the problem lie and where is the elusive answer?

The problem is people, too many of them worldwide. Human overpopulation of the planet earth serves as the largest contributor to our air pollution woes. The first step in reducing the pollution crisis is to reduce the amount of people inhabiting the world.

Population reduction, through various birth control methods, will take a long time. It also will not solve many of the pressing problems that exist at present: global warming through the greenhouse effect; ozone depletion in the stratosphere; ozone in the atmosphere; photochemical smog; acid rain; pesticide and other chemical pollution; nuclear accidents and wastes; and, a new one, radon. Radon is a naturally-occurring gas which is drawn into a home from the underlying soil by air pressure and can cause lung cancer over long periods of exposure.

Since the air is shared by all peoples of the world, the responsibility for the quality of our air lies with all the people of the earth. We all reap the benefits of clean air and suffer under the pain of air pollution. It is, therefore, incumbent upon all of us to ensure the quality of our air for future generations.

How can this be done? Is the problem so big and out of control that it cannot be fixed? No. Since the air pollution problems are the result of human behavior, we can change that behavior to reverse the results. The human being is the only living thing that has the ability to alter its environment.

Where should we begin and what can we presume? We should start by understanding that each individual person has a stake in the future of this planet and, because of this, that person must do his or her part in moving to solve the environmental problems that face us. Once each person accepts this responsibility, we can start to work together as a whole to reverse the conditions that have brought us to this point.

For starters, we can put pressure on our government leaders to create and enforce strict antipollution laws, with severe penalties for those who refuse to comply. If your representatives in government fail to bring about these changes, then use your voting power and campaign for people who will. If an industry or industries fail to comply with government regulations, we can boycott the products. It may cost manufacturers more to produce a product under pollution-free conditions, but they will happily do this if the alternative is no sales.

Special taxes imposed on those responsible for producing chlorofluorocarbons, carbon dioxide emissions, and other pollutants might encourage the search for alternative sources of energy, as well as enforce energy conservation. Increased funding for further energy research would also stimulate further development of alternatives.

Pressure could be brought to bear on foreign governments who refuse to comply with worldwide environmental regulations, such as the cutting or burning of the world's rain forests. These governments can be made to realize that they have no other choice but to comply or become outlaws in the world community.

The sooner a great effort is made by all countries of the world to develop and use alternate forms of energy for fossil fuels and nuclear fission, the sooner we will have clean air. Fusion, solar energy, and a methane recovery program would help to relieve the stress of fossil fuel pollution. Money must be made available for the research and development of this and other clean and safe forms of energy.

Finally, all people in the world should continue the attempt to reduce the growth of the human population. Each country should make zero population growth its ultimate goal. Only by doing this can we preserve the quality of life.

In the words of the cartoonist Walt Kelly, "We have met the enemy and he is us." Although nature does contribute a goodly amount to our air pollution problems, it is the behavior of people that pushes the problems to crisis proportions. Today, we hover on the brink of decision, a decision that will determine the future quality of life for many generations to come. That decision is either to stop polluting and clean up the air or to force our children and grandchildren to suffer the consequences.

Glossary

acid rain—Rainwater containing acids that have formed from the combination of sulfur dioxide, nitric oxide, or nitrogen dioxide gases with water vapor.

aerosol—Refers to particles so tiny that they stay afloat in the air for long periods of time.

air—The colorless, odorless, and tasteless mixture of gases closest to the earth's surface.

alga—A simple plant that contains chlorophyll and photosynthesizes.

amino acid—An organic compound formed from an amino group (NH_2) and a carboxylic acid group (COOH). An essential component of the protein molecule.

anaerobic bacteria—A microorganism able to live in the absence of oxygen.

atmosphere—The primary layer of gases surrounding the earth. The atmosphere extends approximately 600 miles (965 kilometers) above the earth's surface and exerts 14.7 pounds of pressure per square inch at sea level.

biome—The community of living organisms of a single major ecological region.

biosphere—The portion of the earth and its atmosphere that is capable of supporting life.

carbon dioxide (CO_2)—A colorless, odorless, and tasteless gas found naturally in the air (.035%). An excess of this gas, emitted from the burning of fossil fuels, is largely responsible for the greenhouse effect and global warming.

carbon monoxide (CO)—A colorless, odorless, and tasteless gas resulting from the incomplete combustion of fossil fuels.

chlorofluorocarbons—A group of chemical compounds which were widely used as propellants for aerosol spray cans. These compounds are greatly responsible for the depletion of the ozone layer in the stratosphere.

complete combustion—The complete burning of a fossil fuel. The by-products of complete combustion are carbon dioxide and water vapor and oxides of other elements.

coal—One of the three major fossil fuels; used mainly to provide energy for electrical power plants.

convection—The movement of air created by temperature. Cold air falls and pushes the warmer, lighter air up.

DDT, Dichloro-diphenyl-trichloroethane (($ClC_6H_4)_2CHCCl_3$)— A colorless, odorless, and water-insoluble crystalline, which is toxic to humans and other animals when swallowed or absorbed through the skin.

ecology—The study of how all organisms interrelate to each other and their nonliving environment.

emission—The release of waste products during the combustion of fossil fuels.

fallout—Minute particles of radioactive debris which fall slowly through the atmosphere.

fission—A nuclear reaction in which an atomic nucleus splits into fragments, creating a chain reaction that releases heat and light energy.

food chain—The transfer of food energy between organisms within a community. Producers (the autotrophic organisms) generate food in the form of sugars, while the herbivores, carnivores, omnivores, and decomposers (the heterotrophic organisms) transfer and transform this energy until it is finally returned to the carbon or nitrogen cycles.

fossil fuels—Any fuel derived from the fossil remains of plants or animals; e.g., coal, oil, natural gas.

fungus—Plants lacking chlorophyll, and ranging from a single to a multiple-celled organism.

fusion—A nuclear reaction in which the nuclei combine to form a massive nuclei. This crushing or fusing releases large amounts of heat and light energy.

gaseous—Refers to anything in the form of a gas; e.g., gaseous pollution of the air.

global warming—The rising of the earth's mean (average) temperature created by the greenhouse effect.

greenhouse effect—The sequence comprising the absorption of radiation by the earth and the blocking of the heat loss from this radiation by various gases (carbon dioxide, ozone, etc.), resulting in a steady, gradual rise in the temperature of the atmosphere.

groundwater—Water standing in or moving through the soil and underlying strata.

halons—A group of chemicals often used in fire-fighting equipment.

He-3—A chemical produced by the sun and found on the surface of the moon, which may be used as a fuel for nuclear fusion.

hydrologic cycle—The cycle of movement of water from the atmosphere by precipitation to the earth, and its return to the atmosphere by evaporation and transpiration.

incomplete combustion—This occurs when gasoline or other fossil fuels are not burned completely. Incomplete combustion at high temperatures results in the release of certain chemicals which, in the presence of air and sunlight, form the ingredients for photochemical smog.

internal combustion engine—An engine in which fuel is burned within the engine proper, rather than in an external furnace; e.g., gasoline piston engine, diesel engine.

ions—Electrically charged particles.

ionosphere—Also referred to as thermosphere. The ionosphere extends fifty to three hundred miles above the earth's surface. In this layer, gases of the atmosphere are broken into individual electrically charged particles, called ions.

isotope—One of two or more atoms, the nuclei of which have the same number of protons but different numbers of neutrons.

lichen—An alga and a fungus joined in symbiosis (mutualism).

matter—Anything that has weight and takes up space.

methyl chloroform—An industrial solvent which, when released into the atmosphere, contributes to the depletion of the ozone layer in the stratosphere.

mutualism—A symbiotic relationship in which two organisms benefit one another; e.g., the bees and the flower.

natural gas—A fossil fuel derived from the remains of fossilized minute animals.

natural pollution—Air pollution that occurs as the result of natural phenomena.

nitrogen (N)—A gas that makes up 78 percent of the air.

nitric oxide (NO)—A compound formed by the incomplete combustion of fossil fuel; one of the ingredients of photochemical smog.

nitrogen dioxide (NO₂)—A compound formed by the combustion of fossil fuel; one of the ingredients of photochemical smog.

nuclear—Of or concerning atomic nuclei.

oil—A fossil fuel derived from the fossilized remains of minute animals. Also called petroleum.

organism—Any living thing.

oxygen (O₂)—A gas that makes up 21 percent of the air.

ozone (O₃)—An active form of oxygen.

PAN—Peroxyacetyl nitrate, one of the ingredients of photochemical smog.

particulate—Refers to particles in the air.

pesticide—Any chemical that is used to kill pests, especially insects, fungi, and rodents.

pH scale—A scale for measuring the acidity or alkalinity of substances.

photochemical smog—A virulent vapor produced by the incomplete combustion of fossil fuels; mainly composed of PAN, ozone, and carbon monoxide.

plutonium (Pu)—A naturally radioactive element occurring in uranium ore and produced artificially by neutron bombardment of uranium; a radiological poison specifically absorbed by the bone marrow; used as a reactor fuel and in nuclear weapons.

pollutant—Anything that pollutes, especially any gaseous, chemical, or organic waste that contaminates the air, water, or soil.

pollute—To dirty or contaminate.

pollution—The state of being impure or contaminated.

radiation—The emission of radioactive waves or particles.

radioactive cesium (Cs) 137—An extremely virulent form of radiation formed in nuclear reactors.

radon (Rn)—A colorless, radioactive, and inert gaseous element formed by the disintegration of radium.

reactor (nuclear)—Any of several devices in which a chain reaction is initiated and controlled, with the consequent production of heat energy.

solar energy—Energy obtained directly from the sun.

stratosphere—The layer of gases that is anywhere from ten to forty miles above the earth's surface. It contains the protective ozone layer that surrounds the earth.

sulfur dioxide (SO_2)—A compound formed both naturally and by the combustion of coal or oil, containing sulfur. When combined with water vapor, it forms sulfurous acid (H_2SO_3), the main ingredient of acid rain.

sulfurous acid (H_2SO_3)—Formed when sulfur dioxide gas combines with water vapor; the main ingredient of acid rain.

technology—The application of science to industry.

temperature inversion—An increase in the air temperature with an increase of altitude, instead of the normal decrease.

thermosphere—Another name for ionosphere.

troposphere—The layer of gases closest to the earth's surface.

uranium (U) 235—The uranium isotope with the mass number of 235; fissionable; with slow neutrons and capable in a critical mass of sustaining a chain reaction that can proceed explosively.

uranium (U) 238—The most common isotope of uranium, with the mass number 238; nonfissionable; irradiated with neutrons to produce fissionable plutonium 239.

Further Reading

Acid Rain Reader. Acid Rain Foundation: Raleigh, N.C., 1987.

Asimov, Isaac. *How Did We Find Out about the Atmosphere?* Walker and Co.: New York, 1985.

Dolan, Edward F., Jr. *Great Mysteries of the Air.* Putnam: New York, 1983.

Epstein, Samuel S. et al. *Hazardous Waste in America.* Sierra Club: San Francisco, 1982.

Genzelman, Stanley David. *The Science of Wonder of the Atmosphere.* Wiley: New York, 1980.

Miller, Christina G. and Louise A. Berry. *Acid Rain.* Messner: New York, 1986.

Neiburger, Melvin. *Understanding Our Atmosphere's Environment.* W. H. Freeman: New York, 1982.

For Further Information

Government Agencies

Agency for Toxic Substances and Disease Registry
1600 Clifton Road NE
Atlanta, GA 30333

Centers for Disease Control
1600 Clifton Road NE
Atlanta, GA 30333

Department of Energy
1000 Independence Avenue SW
Washington, DC 20585

Department of the Interior
1800 D Street NW
Washington, DC 20240

Environmental Protection Agency
Public Information Center
401 M Street SW
Washington, DC 20460

The National Environmental Satellite Data and Information Service
1825 Connecticut Avenue
Washington, DC 20235

National Institutes of Health
(includes National Cancer
Institute; National Heart, Lung,
and Blood Institute; National
Institute of Allergy and Infectious
Diseases)
9000 Rockville Pike
Bethesda, MD 20892

Nuclear Regulatory
Commission
1717 H Street NW
Washington, DC 20555

Office of Science and
Technology Policy
Old Executive Office Building
Washington, DC 20506

Consumer Groups

Environmental Action
Foundation
724 Dupont Circle Building NW
Washington, DC 20036

Environmental Defense Fund
1525 18th Street NW
Washington, DC 20036

Greenpeace Action
96 Spring Street
New York, NY 10014

Natural Resources Defense
Council
Suite 300
1350 New York Avenue NW
Washington, DC 20005

Public Citizen Health Research
Group
200 P Street NW
Washington, DC 20036

World Watch Institute
460 Park Avenue South
New York, NY 10016

Index

About the Author

Martin J. Gutnik is a science teacher, specializing in environmental science, and the author of a number of books for young people. He has also lectured on ecology and the environment in greater Milwaukee and Chicago. Mr. Gutnik lives in Wisconsin with his family.